EASY GUITAR
WITH NOTES & TAB

THE OFFSPRING
GREATEST HITS

All songs written by Dexter Holland
Underachiever Music (BMI)
International Copyright Secured
All Rights Reserved

ISBN 978-0-634-08187-3

HAL•LEONARD®
CORPORATION
7777 W. BLUEMOUND RD. P.O. BOX 13819 MILWAUKEE, WI 53213

Visit Hal Leonard Online at
www.halleonard.com

CONTENTS

STRUM AND PICK PATTERNS

This chart contains the suggested strum and pick patterns that are referred to by number at the beginning of each song in this book. The symbols ⊓ and ∨ in the strum patterns refer to down and up strokes, respectively. The letters in the pick patterns indicate which right-hand fingers plays which strings.

p = thumb
i = index finger
m = middle finger
a = ring finger

For example; Pick Pattern 2
is played: thumb - index - middle - ring

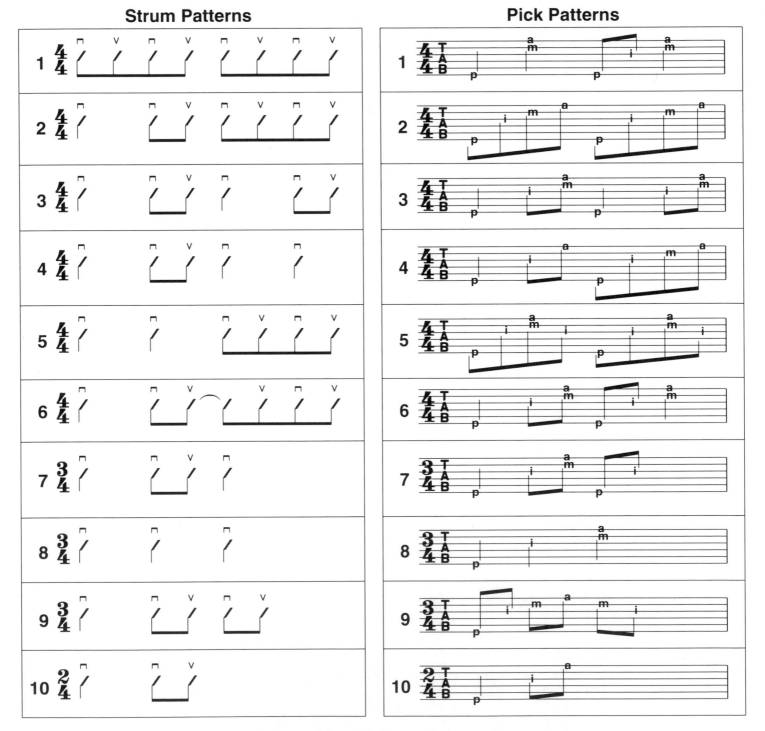

Strum Patterns   **Pick Patterns**

You can use the 3/4 Strum or Pick Patterns in songs written in compound meter (6/8, 9/8, 12/8, etc.).
For example, you can accompany a song in 6/8 by playing the 3/4 pattern twice in each measure.
The 4/4 Strum and Pick Patterns can be used for songs written in cut time (¢) by doubling the note
time values in the patterns. Each pattern would therefore last two measures in cut time.

Can't Repeat

Words and Music by Dexter Holland

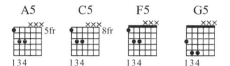

Strum Pattern: 4
Pick Pattern: 1

Intro
Fast Rock

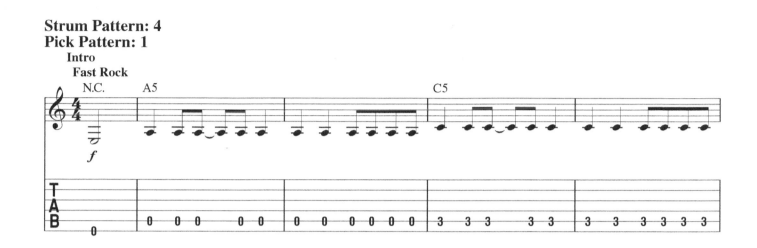

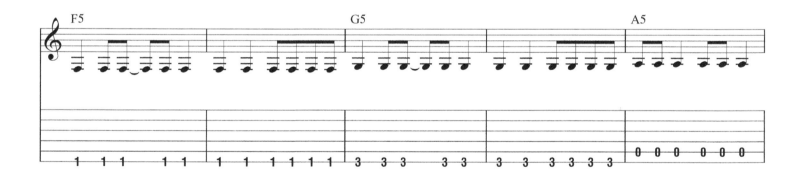

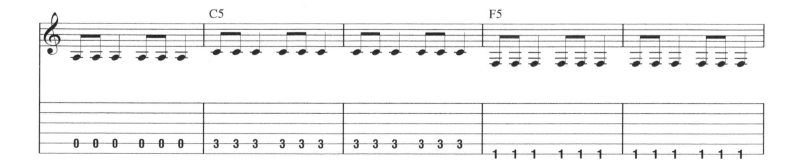

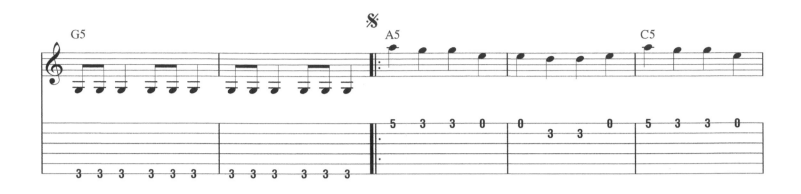

To Coda 1

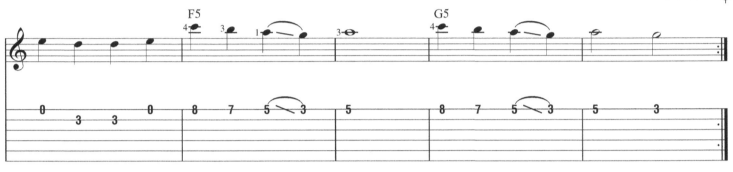

Verse

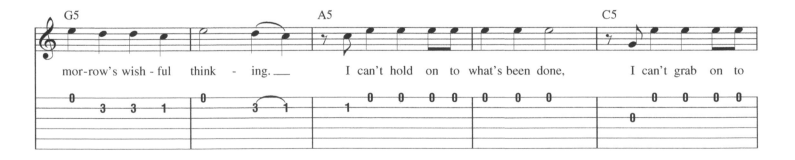

1. I woke the oth-er day and saw my world has changed. The past is o - ver, but to -
2. *See additional lyrics*

mor-row's wish-ful think - ing.___ I can't hold on to what's been done, I can't grab on to

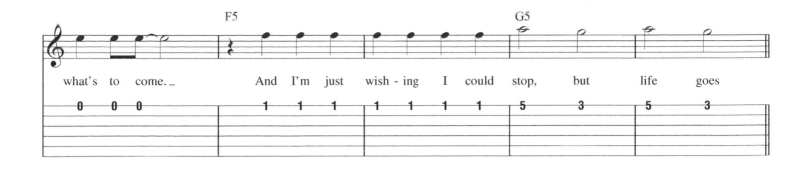

what's to come. ___ And I'm just wish-ing I could stop, but life goes

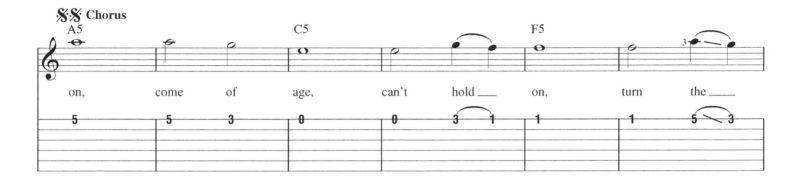

𝄋𝄋 **Chorus**

on, come of age, can't hold ___ on, turn the ___

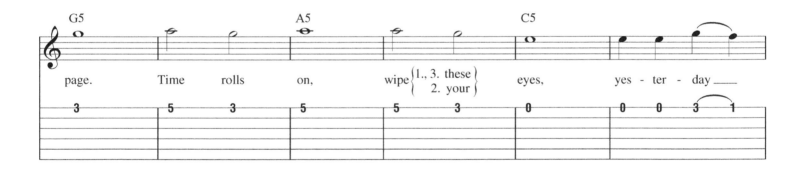

page. Time rolls on, wipe {1., 3. these / 2. your} eyes, yes-ter-day ___

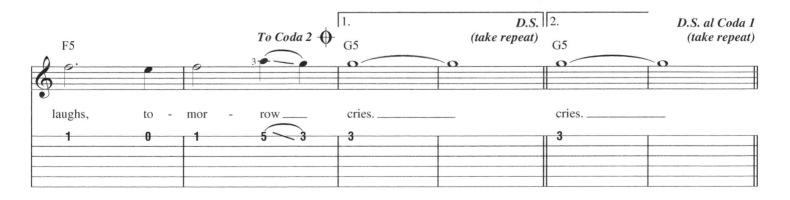

laughs, to-mor-row ___ cries. ___ cries. ___

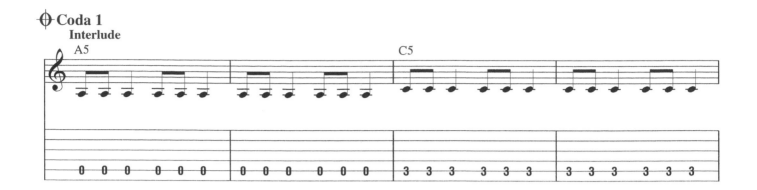

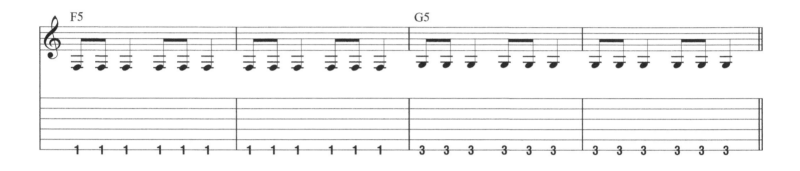

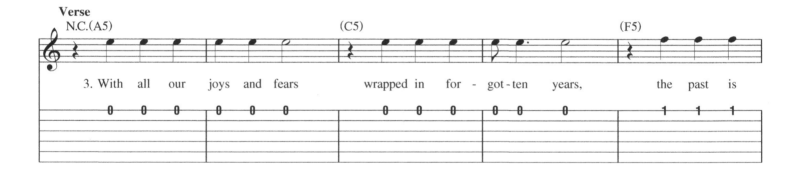

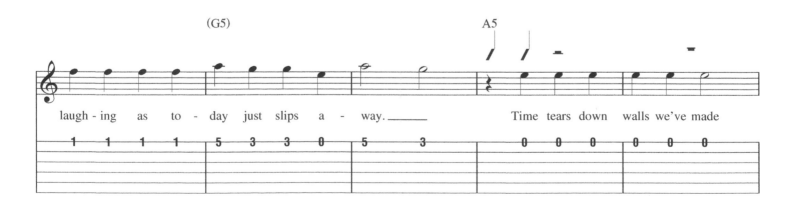

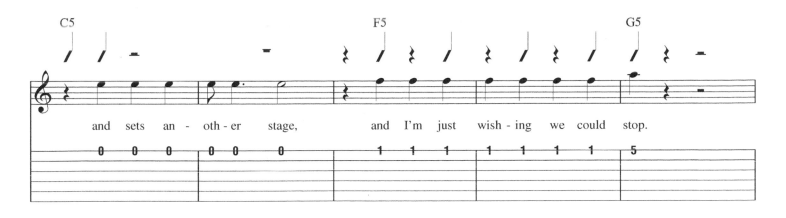

and sets an‑oth‑er stage, and I'm just wish‑ing we could stop.

Coda 2

D.S.S al Coda 2

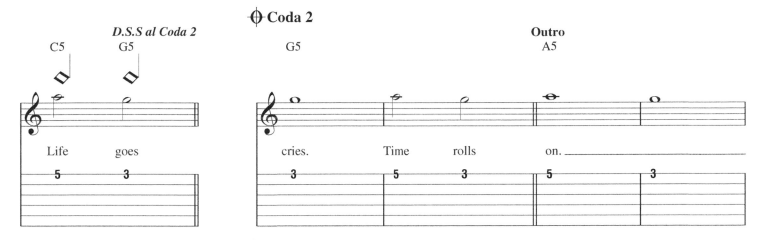

Life goes cries. Time rolls on.

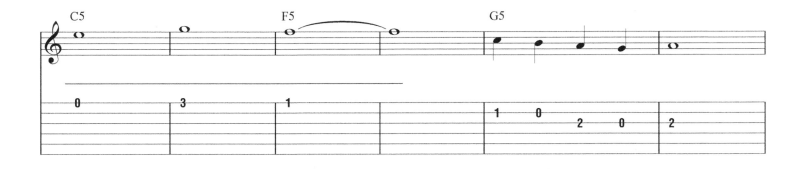

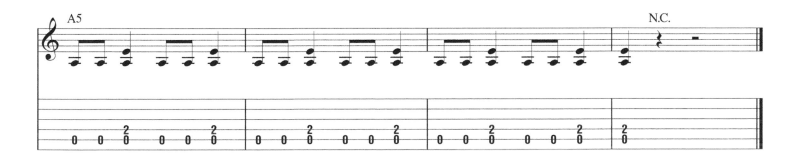

Additional Lyrics

2. Memories are bittersweet, the good times we can't repeat.
   Those days are gone and we can never get 'em back.
   Now we must move ahead, despite our fear and dread.
   We're all just wishing we could stop, but life goes...

Come Out and Play

Words and Music by Dexter Holland

pay no mind. If you're un - der eigh - teen, you won't be do - ing an - y time. _____

Hey, _____ come out and play. _

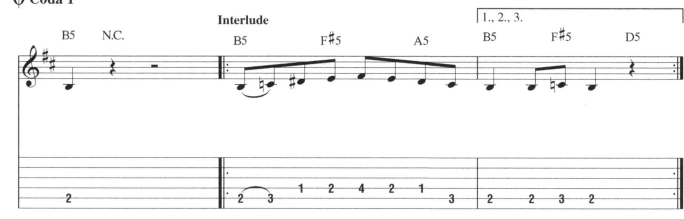

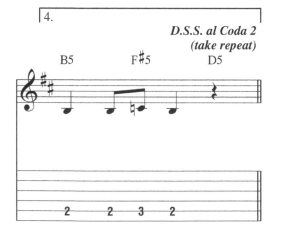

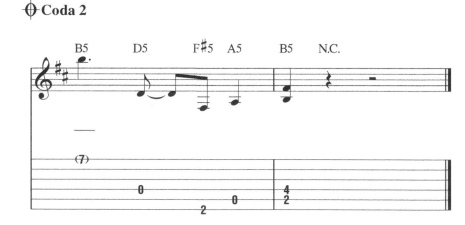

Additional Lyrics

2. By the time you hear the siren
It's already too late.
One goes to the morgue and the other to jail.
One guy's wasted and the other's a waste.

Pre-Chorus 2., 3. It goes down the same as the thousand before.
No one's getting smarter, no one's learning the score.
Your never ending spree of death and violence and hate
Is gonna tie your own rope, tie your own rope, tie your own...

Self Esteem

Words and Music by Dexter Holland

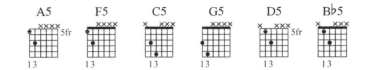

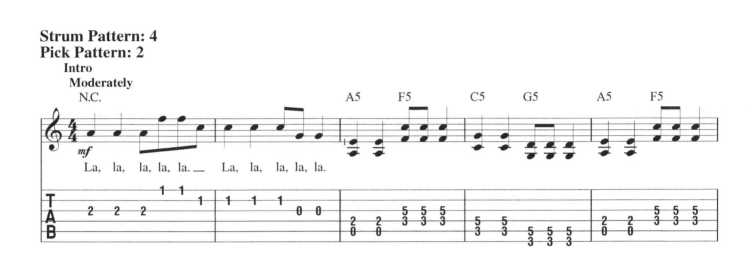

Strum Pattern: 4
Pick Pattern: 2
Intro
Moderately

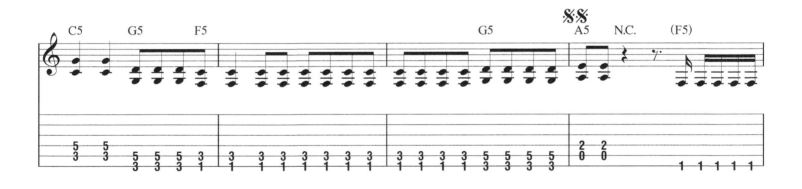

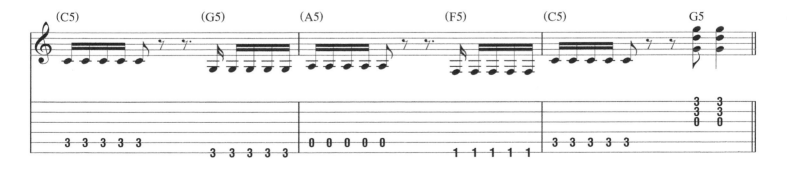

Verse

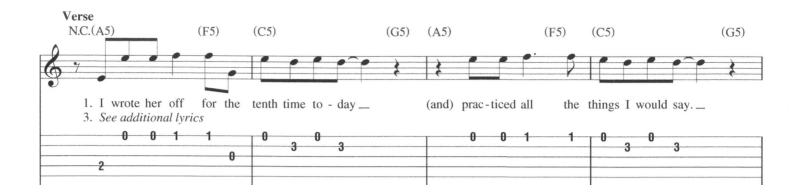

1. I wrote her off for the tenth time to-day __ (and) prac-ticed all the things I would say. __
3. *See additional lyrics*

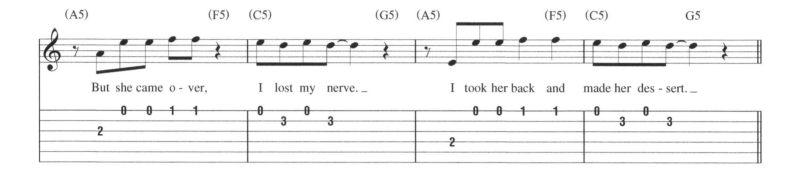

But she came o-ver, I lost my nerve. __ I took her back and made her des-sert. __

Pre-Chorus

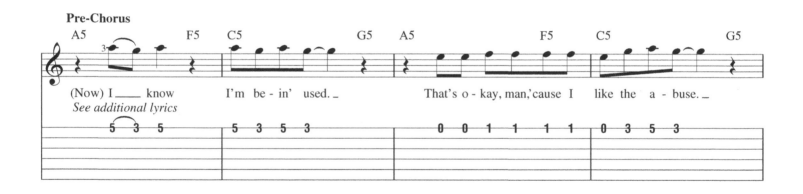

(Now) I __ know I'm be-in' used. __ That's o-kay, man,'cause I like the a-buse. __
See additional lyrics

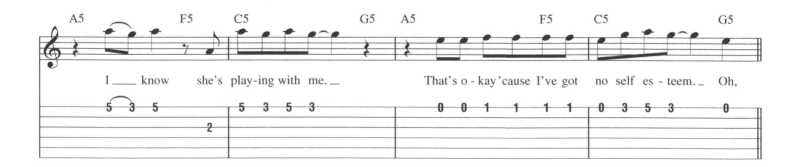

I __ know she's play-ing with me. __ That's o-kay 'cause I've got no self es-teem. __ Oh,

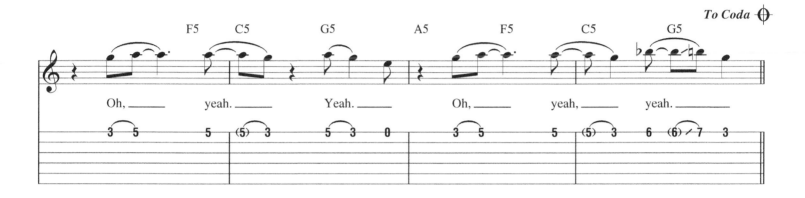

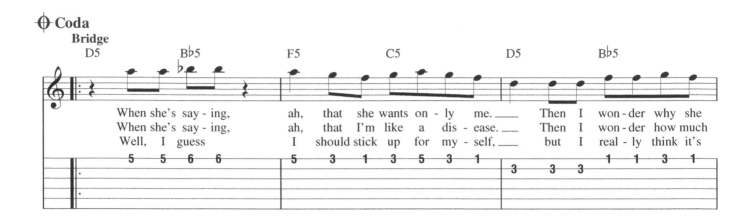

When she's say - ing, ah, that she wants on - ly me. ____ Then I won - der why she
When she's say - ing, ah, that I'm like a dis - ease. ____ Then I won - der how much
Well, I guess I should stick up for my - self, ____ but I real - ly think it's

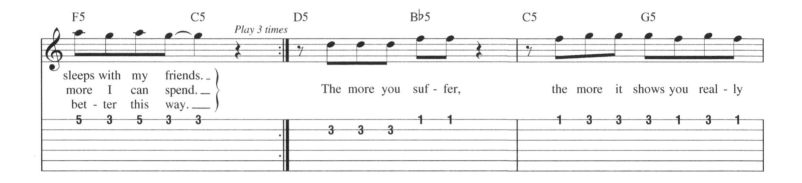

Play 3 times

sleeps with my friends. ____
more I can spend. ____
bet - ter this way. ____

The more you suf - fer, the more it shows you real - ly

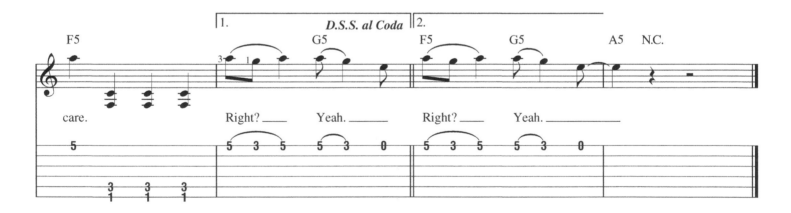

D.S.S. al Coda

care. Right? ____ Yeah. ____ Right? ____ Yeah. ____

Additional Lyrics

3. Now I'll relate this little bit
   That happens more than I'd like to admit.
   Late at night she knocks on my door.
   She's drunk again and looking to score.

Pre-Chorus (Now) I know I should say no,
   But that's kind of hard when she's ready to go.
   I may be dumb, but I'not a dweeb.
   I'm just a sucker with no self esteem.

Gotta Get Away

Words and Music by Dexter Holland

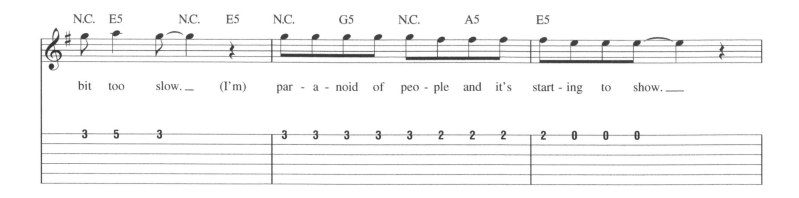

bit too slow. __ (I'm) par - a - noid of peo - ple and it's start - ing to show. __

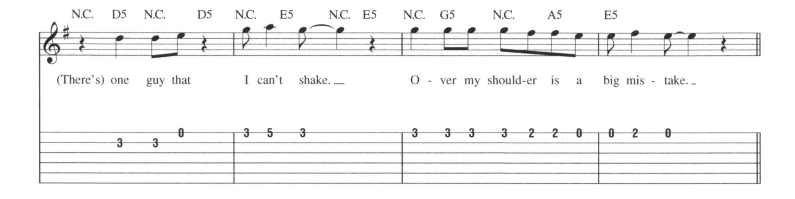

(There's) one guy that I can't shake. __ O - ver my should-er is a big mis - take. _

𝄋 Chorus

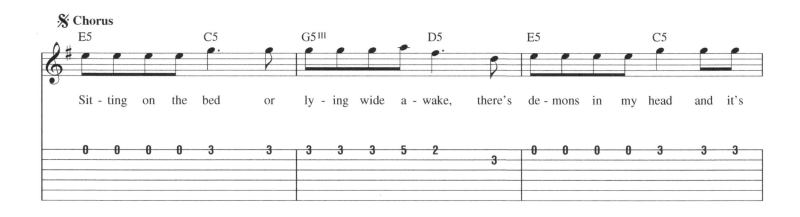

Sit - ting on the bed or ly - ing wide a - wake, there's de - mons in my head and it's

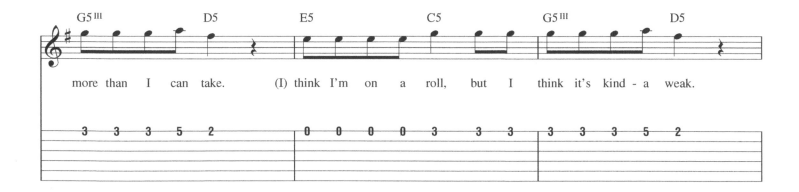

more than I can take. (I) think I'm on a roll, but I think it's kind - a weak.

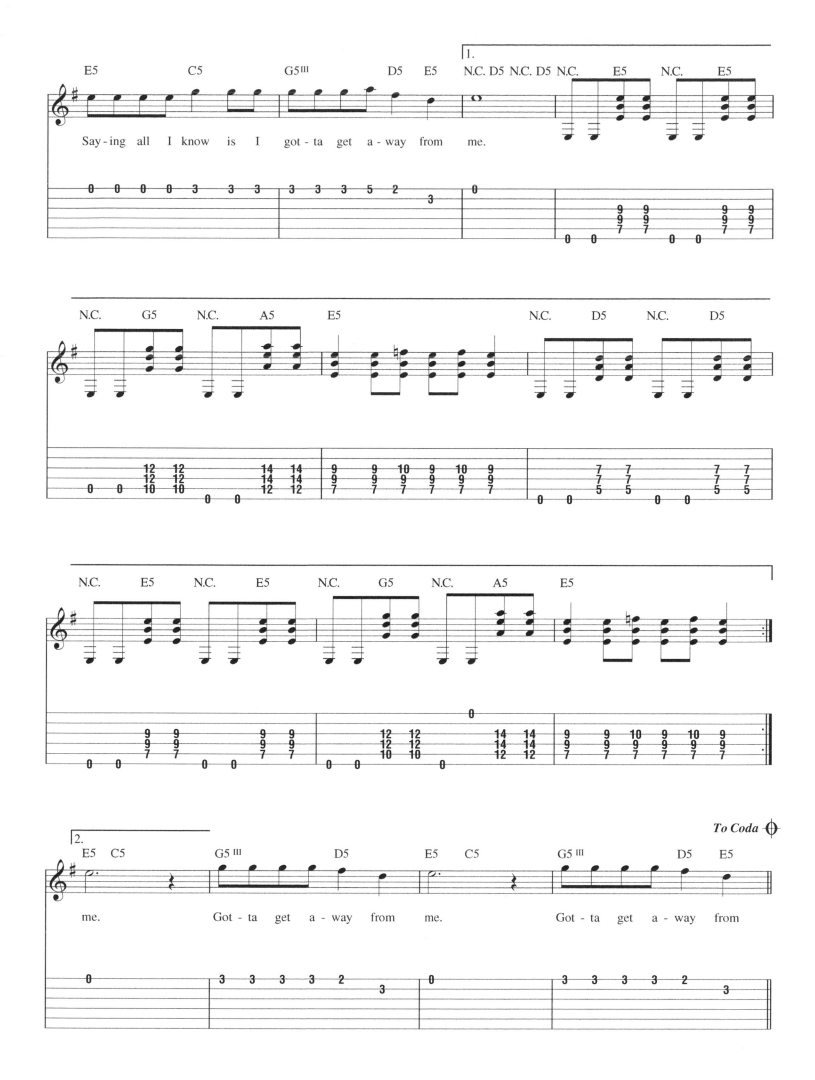

Interlude

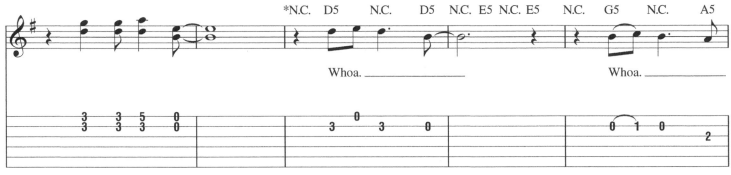

*Intro pattern

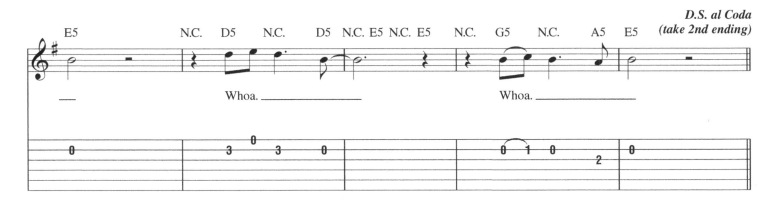

D.S. al Coda
(take 2nd ending)

⊕ **Coda**

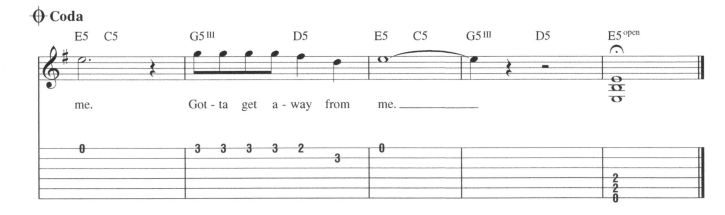

Additional Lyrics

2. I tell you something, just ain't right.
   My head is on loose, but my shoes are tight.
   Avoiding my friends, 'cause they all bug.
   Life is like a riddle and I'm really stumped.
   If you reason, don't you know.
   Your own preoccupation is where you'll go.
   You're being followed, look around.
   It's only my shadow creepin' on the ground.

All I Want

Words and Music by Dexter Holland

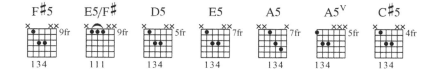

Strum Pattern: 1, 2
Pick Pattern: 4, 5

Intro

Yah, yah, yah, yah, yah.

Verse

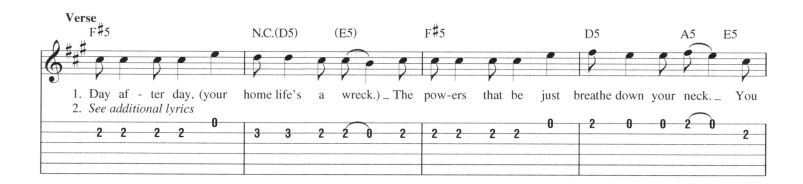

1. Day af - ter day, (your home life's a wreck.)_ The pow-ers that be just breathe down your neck._ You
2. *See additional lyrics*

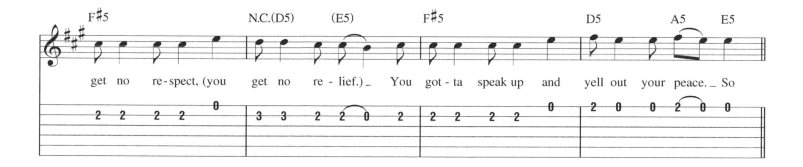

get no re - spect, (you get no re - lief.)_ You got - ta speak up and yell out your peace._ So

Pre-Chorus

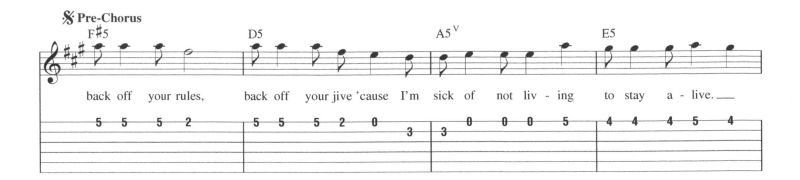

back off your rules, back off your jive 'cause I'm sick of not liv-ing to stay a-live. ___

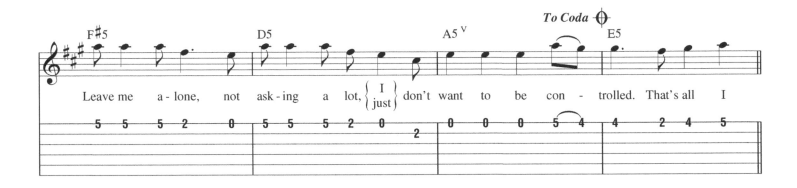

Leave me a-lone, not ask-ing a lot, { I / just } don't want to be con-trolled. That's all I

Chorus

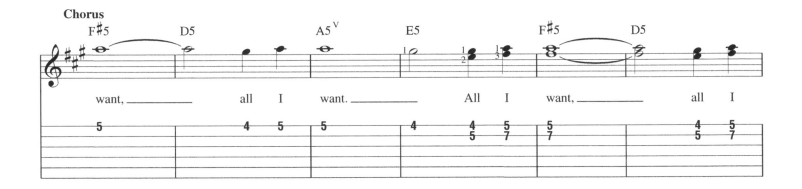

want, _____ all I want. _____ All I want, _____ all I

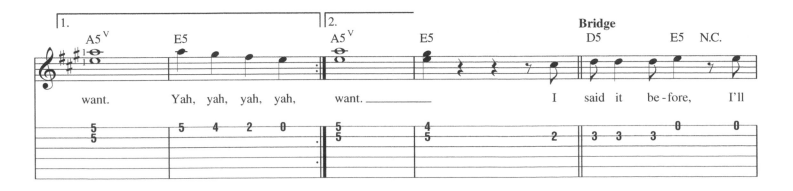

want. Yah, yah, yah, yah, want. _____ I said it be-fore, I'll

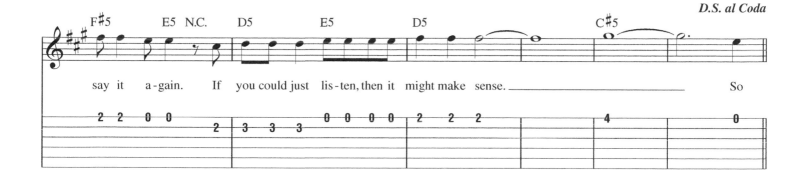

say it a-gain. If you could just lis-ten, then it might make sense._____ So

Coda

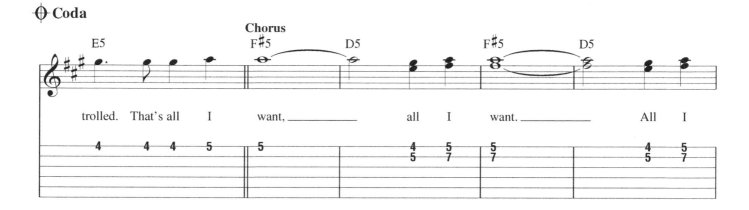

Chorus

trolled. That's all I want,_____ all I want._____ All I

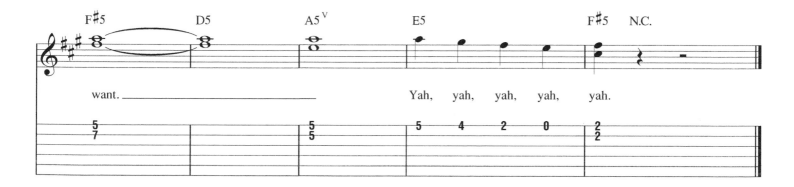

want._____ Yah, yah, yah, yah, yah.

Additional Lyrics

2. How many times (is it gonna take)
Till someone around you hears what you say?
You've tried being cool, (you feel like a lie.)
You've played by their rules, now it's their turn to try.

Gone Away

Words and Music by Dexter Holland

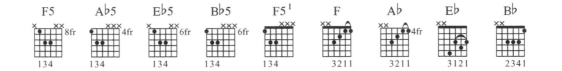

Strum Pattern: 2, 4
Pick Pattern: 3

Intro
Moderate Rock

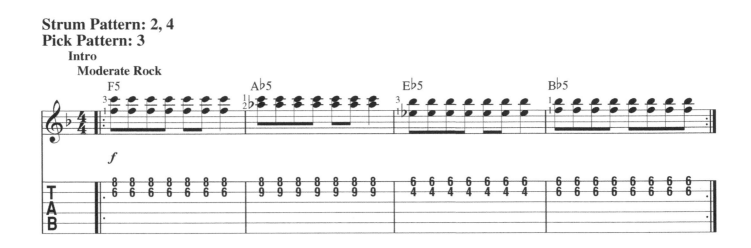

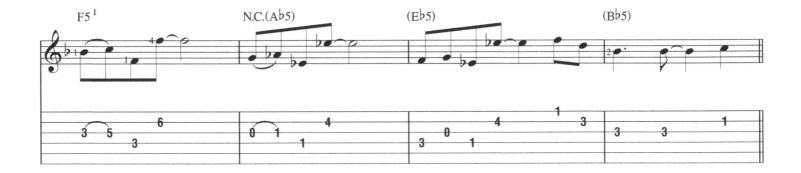

Verse

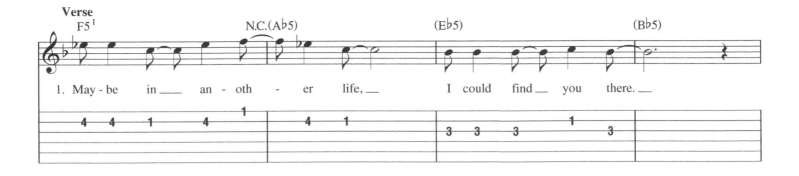

1. May-be in __ an-oth-er life, __ I could find __ you there. __

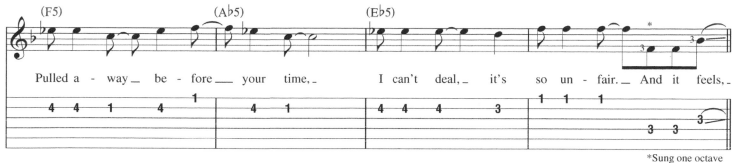

Pulled a - way__ be - fore__ your time,__ I can't deal,__ it's so un - fair. And it feels,__

*Sung one octave
higher, next 8
meas.

Chorus

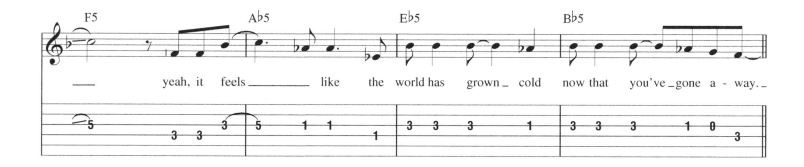

__ and it feels _____ like heav-en's so __ far a - way. _____ And it feels,__

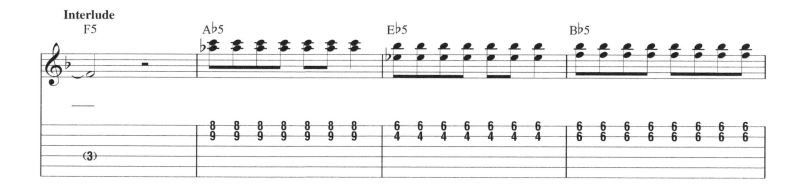

__ yeah, it feels _____ like the world has grown __ cold now that you've __ gone a - way.__

Interlude

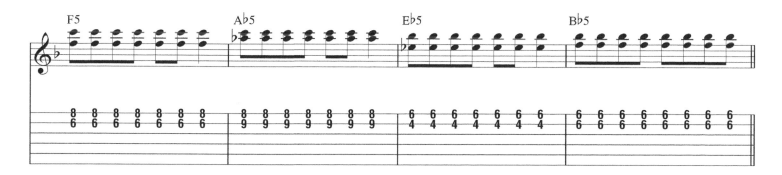

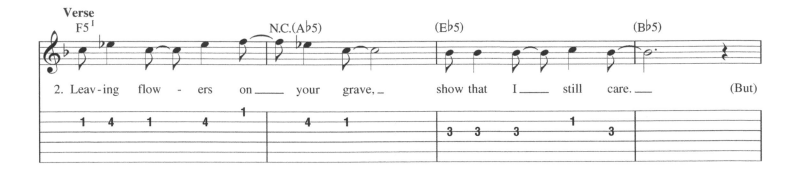

Verse

2. Leav-ing flow - ers on ____ your grave, ____ show that I ____ still care. ____ (But)

black ros - es ____ and Hail ____ Mar - y's ____ can't bring back ____ what's tak - en from ____ me.

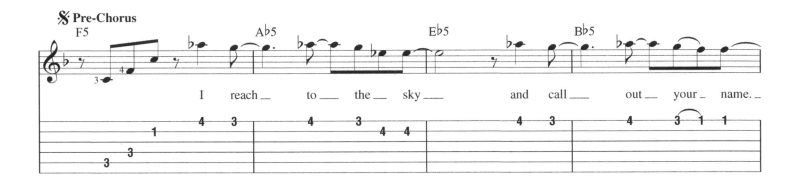

Pre-Chorus

I reach ____ to ____ the ____ sky ____ and call ____ out ____ your ____ name. ____

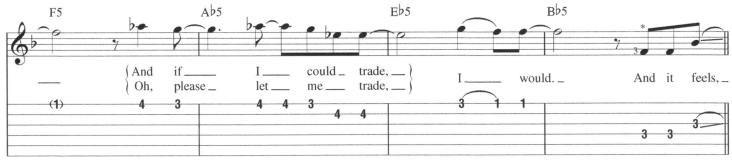

{ And if ____ I ____ could ____ trade, ____ }
{ Oh, please ____ let ____ me ____ trade, ____ }
I ____ would. ____ And it feels, ____

*Sung one octave higher, next 16 meas.

Chorus

To Coda ⊕

____ and it feels ____ like heav-en's so ____ far a - way. ____ And it stings, ____

yeah, it stings ____ now. The world is so ____ cold now that you've ___ gone a - way, ___

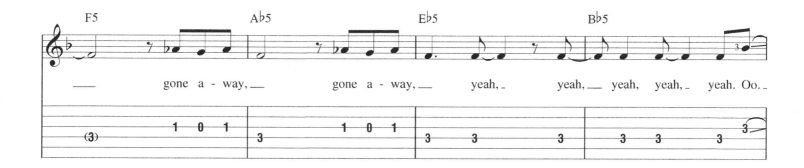

___ gone a - way, ___ gone a - way, ___ yeah, ___ yeah, ___ yeah, yeah, ___ yeah. Oo. ___

___ Well, oo, _____ whoa, _____ yeah. ___

Bridge

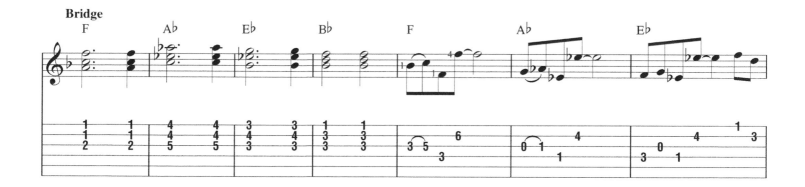

Interlude

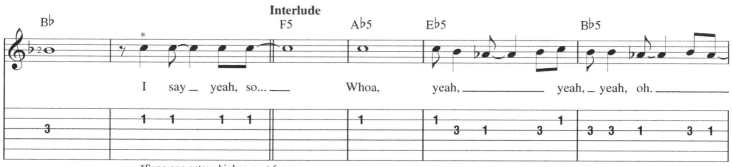

I say ___ yeah, so... ___ Whoa, ___ yeah, _____ yeah, ___ yeah, oh. ___

*Sung one octave higher, next 6 meas.

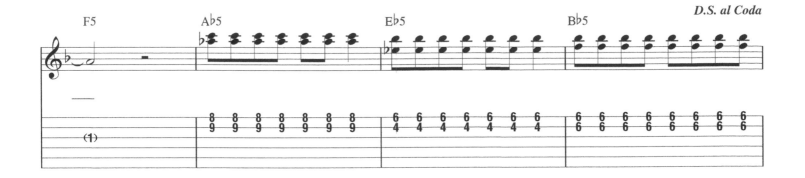

*Sung one octave higher till end

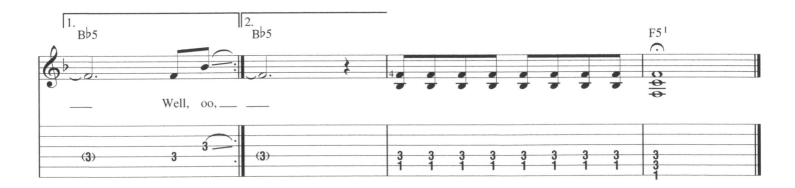

Pretty Fly (For a White Guy)

Words and Music by Dexter Holland

fakes it an - y - way.   He may not have a clue and   he may not have style,   but

ev - 'ry - thing he lacks,   well, he makes up in de - ni - al.   So don't de - bate. __   He's a

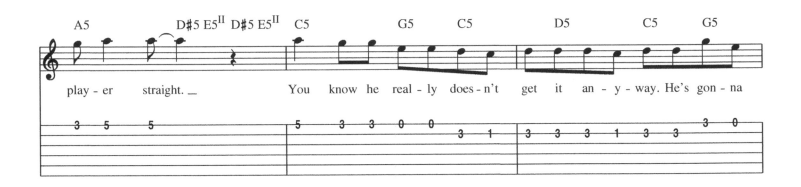

play - er   straight. __   You know he real - ly does - n't get it an - y - way. He's gon - na

play the field __   and keep it real. __   For you no way,   for

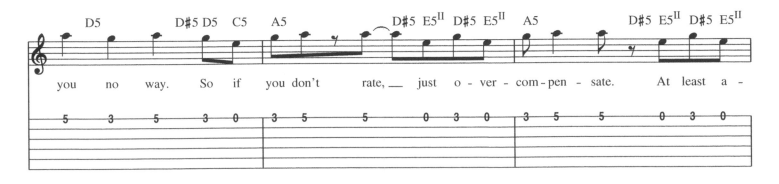

you no way.   So if you don't rate, __ just o - ver - com - pen - sate.   At least a -

you-'ll know you can al-ways go on Rik-ki Lake. The world {needs / loves}

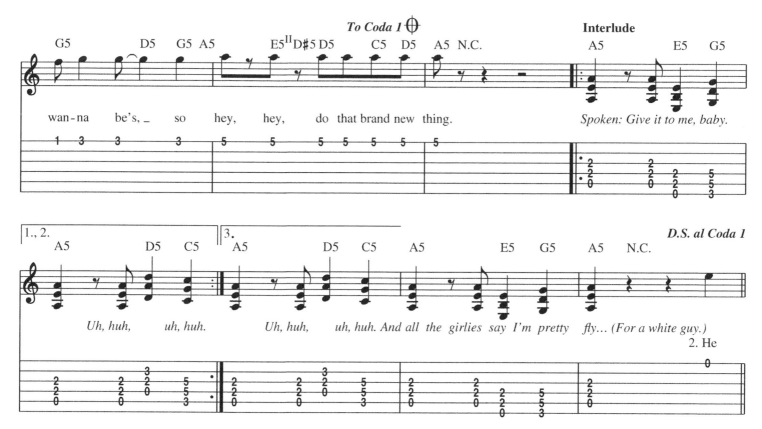

wan-na be's, __ so hey, hey, do that brand new thing. *Spoken: Give it to me, baby.*

Uh, huh, uh, huh. Uh, huh, uh, huh. And all the girlies say I'm pretty fly... (For a white guy.) 2. He

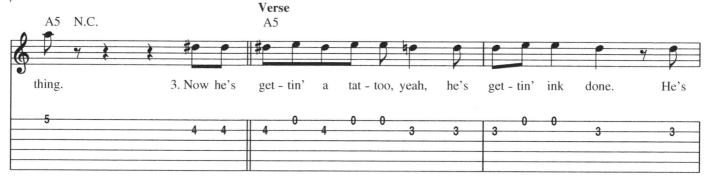

thing. 3. Now he's get-tin' a tat-too, yeah, he's get-tin' ink done. He's

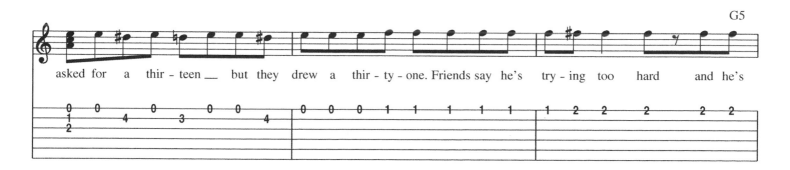

asked for a thir-teen __ but they drew a thir-ty-one. Friends say he's try-ing too hard and he's

Additional Lyrics

2. He needs some cool tunes, not just any will suffice.
   But they didn't have Ice Cube so he bought Vanilla Ice.
   Now cruising in his Pinto, he sees homies as he pass,
   But if he looks twice, they're gonna kick his lily ass.

Why Don't You Get a Job?

Words and Music by Dexter Holland

wants more di - ne - ro just to stay at home. Well, my friend, you got - ta ___ say ___

Chorus

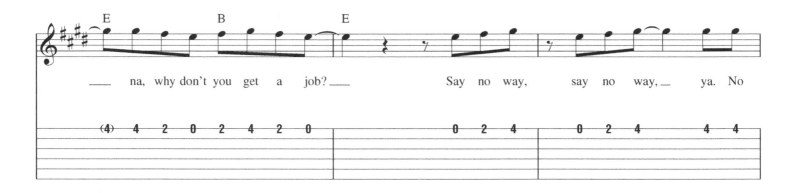

___ I won't pay, I won't pay ___ ya. No way. ___ Na,

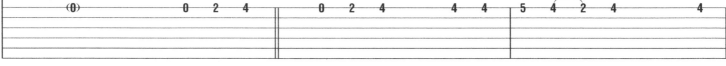

___ na, why don't you get a job? ___ Say no way, say no way, ___ ya. No

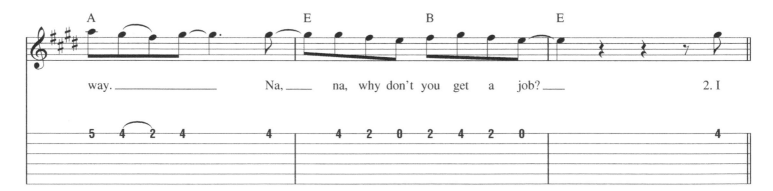

way. ___ Na, ___ na, why don't you get a job? ___ 2. I

𝄋 Verse

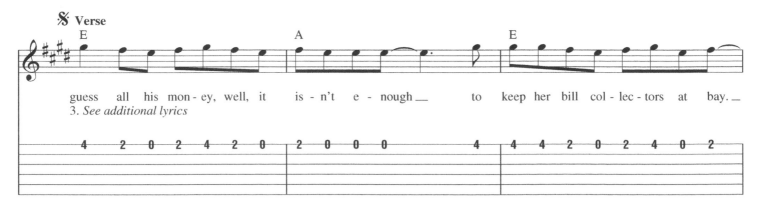

guess all his mon - ey, well, it is - n't e - nough ___ to keep her bill col - lec - tors at bay. ___
3. See additional lyrics

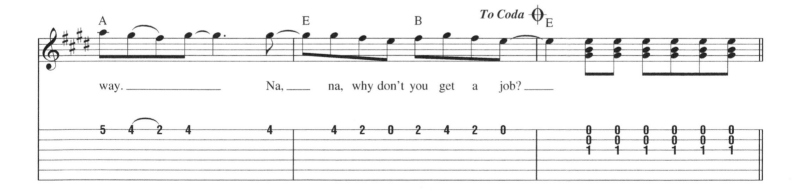

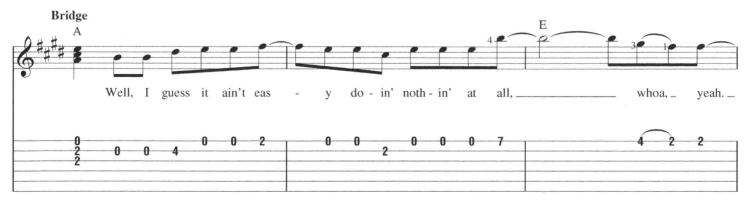

But hey, man, free __ rides just don't come a - long __ ev-'ry day. __

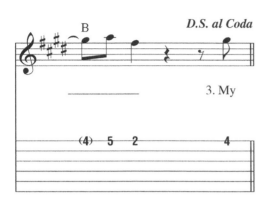

D.S. al Coda

3. My

Coda

Outro

__ I won't give __ you no mon - ey; I

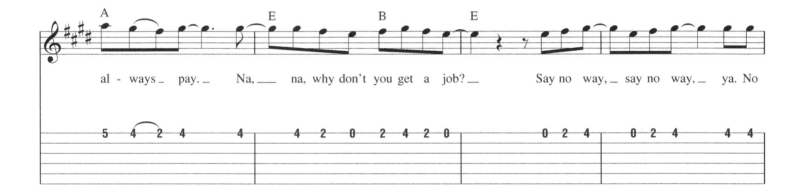

al - ways __ pay. __ Na, __ na, why don't you get a job? __ Say no way, __ say no way, __ ya. No

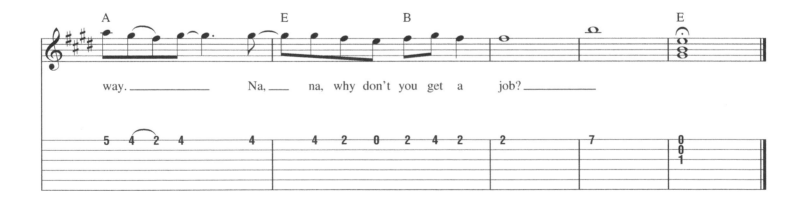

way. _____ Na, __ na, why don't you get a job? _____

Additional Lyrics

3. My friend's got a boyfriend, man she hates that dick.
   She tells me every day.
   He wants more dinero just to stay at home.
   Well, my friend, you gotta say...

The Kids Aren't Alright

Words and Music by Dexter Holland

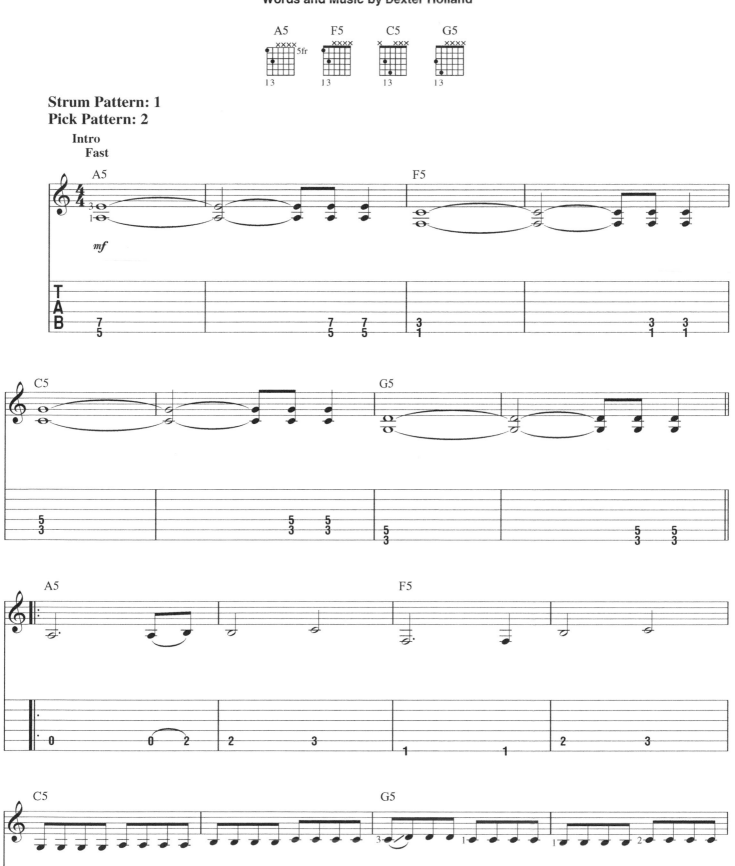

Verse

1. When we were young the fu - ture was so bright, __ the old neigh - bor- hood was
2. *See additional lyrics*

so a - live. __ And ev - 'ry kid on the whole damn street __

was gon - na make it big and not be beat. __ Now the neigh - bor - hood's

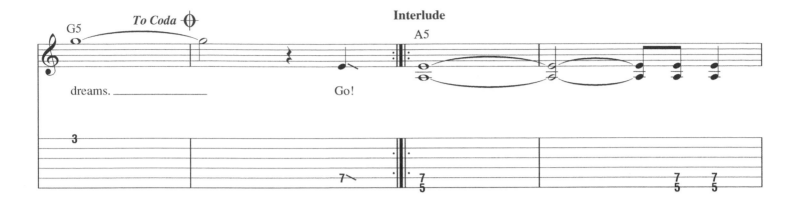

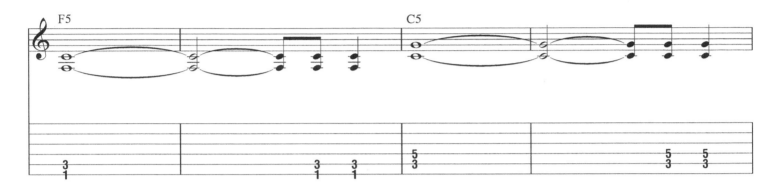

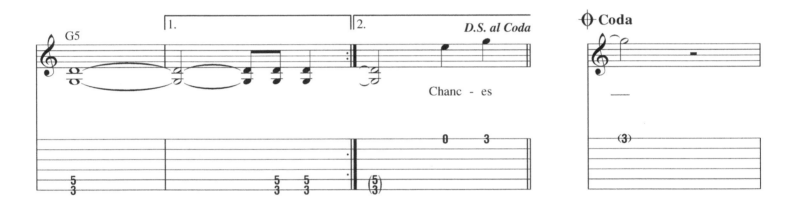

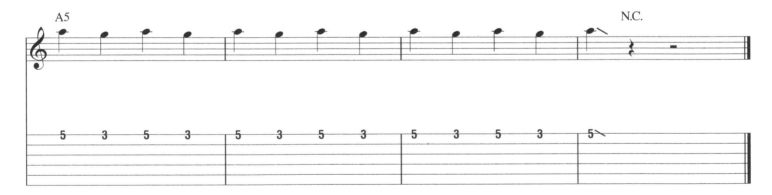

Additional Lyrics

2. Jamie had a chance, well, she really did;
   Instead she dropped out and had a couple of kids.
   Mark still lives at home 'cause he's got no job;
   He just plays guitar and smokes a lot of pot.
   Jay committed suicide,
   Brandon O.D.'d and died.
   What the hell is going on?
   The cruellest dream, reality.

Original Prankster

Words and Music by Dexter Holland

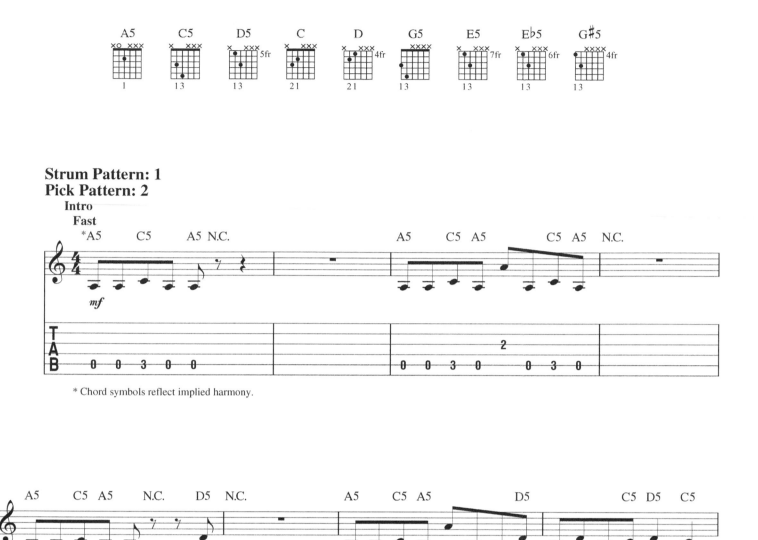

Strum Pattern: 1
Pick Pattern: 2

Intro
Fast

* Chord symbols reflect implied harmony.

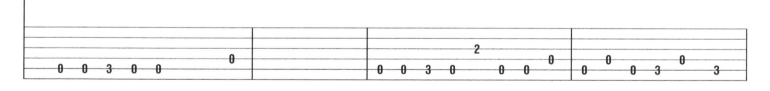

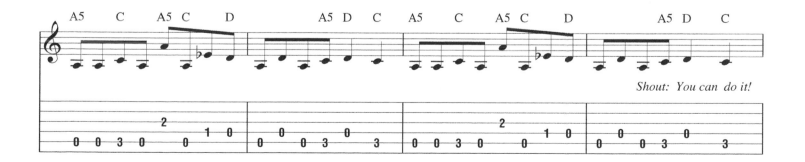

Shout: You can do it!

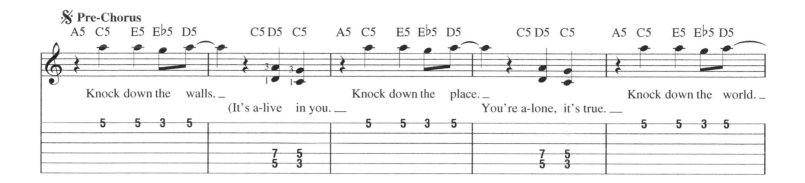

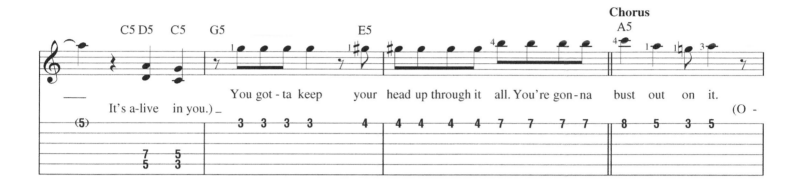

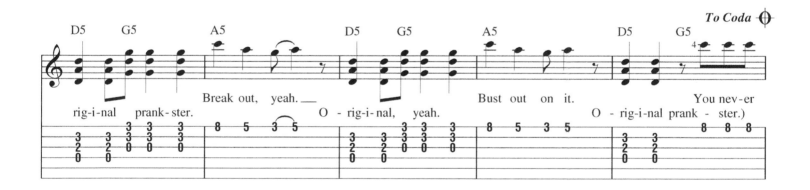

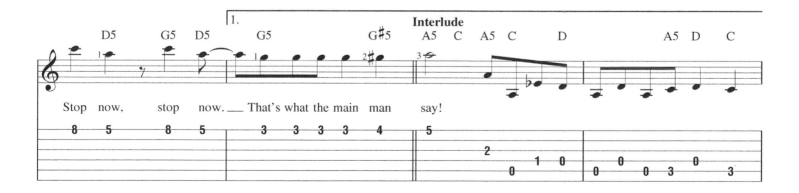

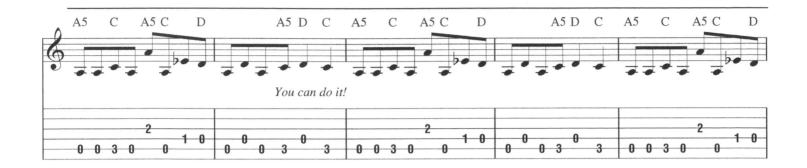

You can do it!

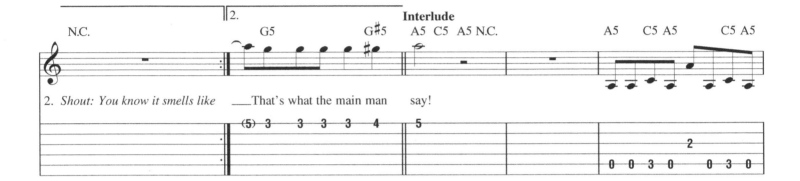

Interlude

2. *Shout: You know it smells like* ___ *That's what the main man say!*

(Hey!)

(You can do it!)

Bridge

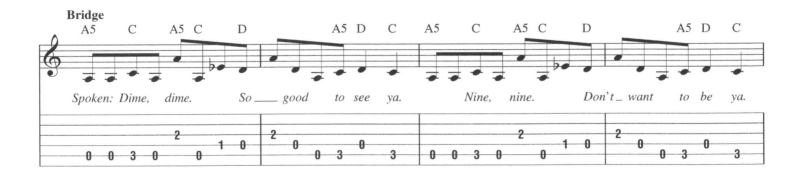

Spoken: Dime, dime. So ___ good to see ya. Nine, nine. Don't _ want to be ya.

Additional Lyrics

2. *Shout: You know it smells like shit. Goddamn.*
   Tag team doubleheader. Son of Sam.
   Fire always makes it better.
   Navigate with style and aplomb
   'Cause wherever you're at, that's the tip you's on.
   Lies, lies. Says he's down in the Bahamas.
   Tries, tries. Bangin' little hoochie mamas.
   No way. None of this is true.
   Well, he'll see there comes a day when the joke's on you, yeah.

Want You Bad

Words and Music by Dexter Holland

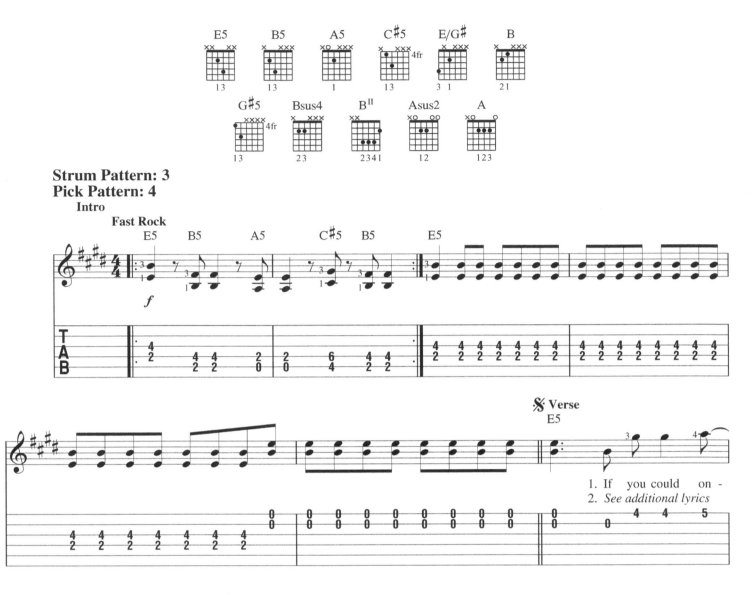

Strum Pattern: 3
Pick Pattern: 4

Intro
Fast Rock

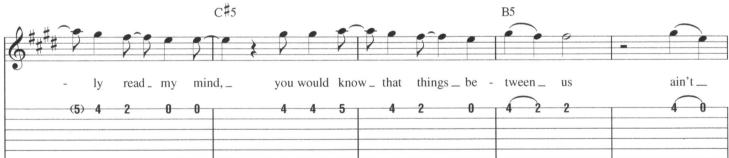

1. If you could on -
2. *See additional lyrics*

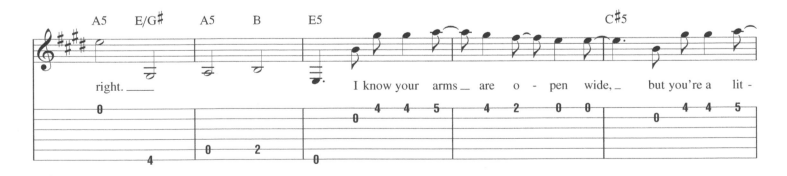

- ly read my mind, you would know that things be - tween us ain't right.

I know your arms are o - pen wide, but you're a lit -

-tle on the straight side. I can't lie.

Pre-Chorus

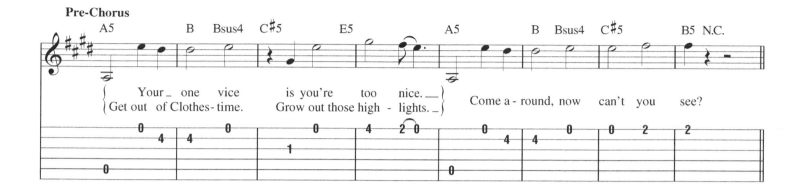

{ Your one vice is you're too nice.
{ Get out of Clothes-time. Grow out those high - lights.

Come a - round, now can't you see?

Chorus

To Coda ⊕

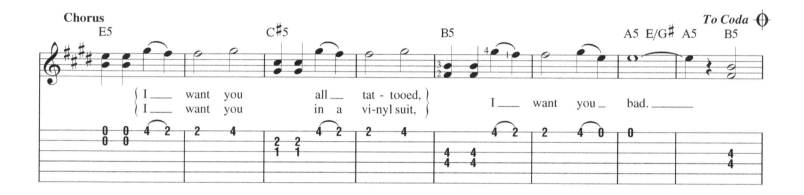

{ I want you all tat - tooed,
{ I want you all in a vi-nyl suit,

I want you bad.

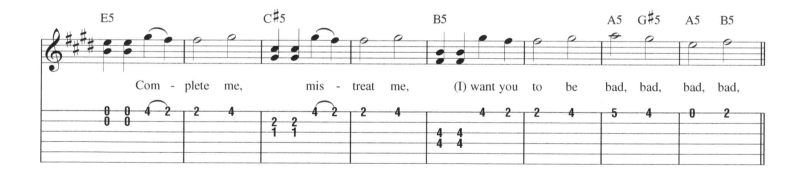

Com - plete me, mis - treat me, (I) want you to be bad, bad, bad, bad,

Interlude

D.S. al Coda

bad.

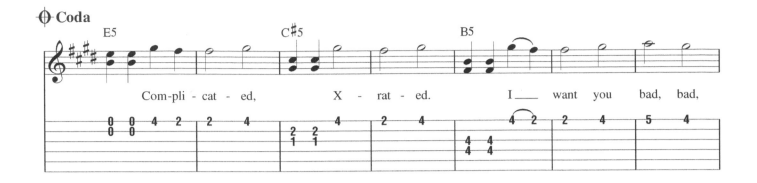

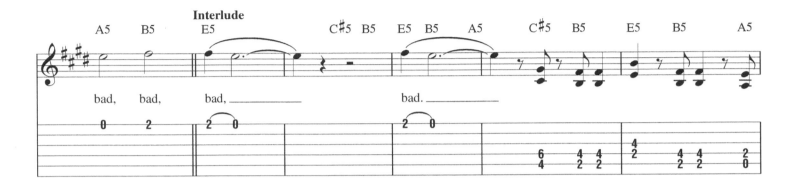

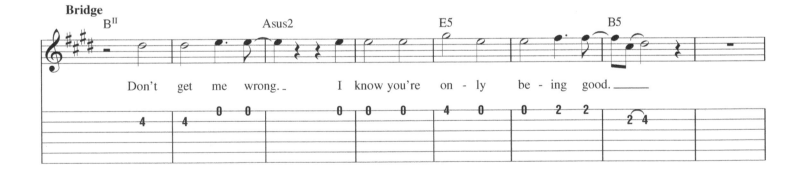

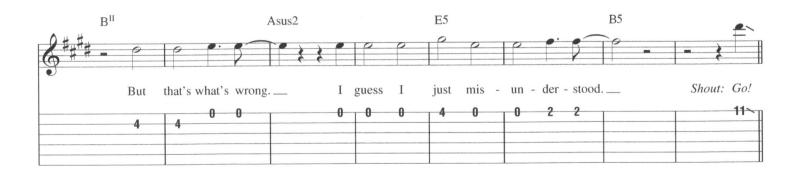

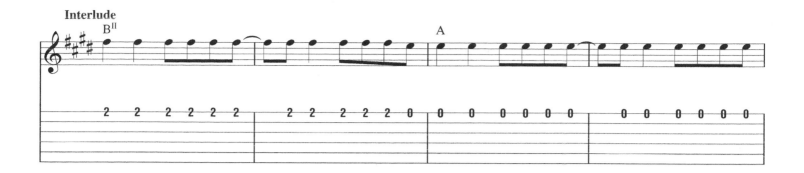
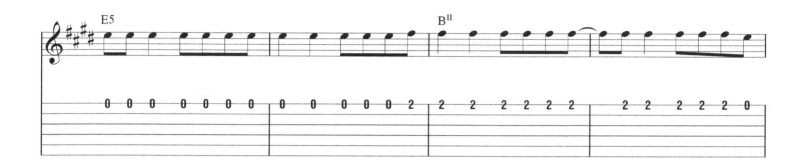
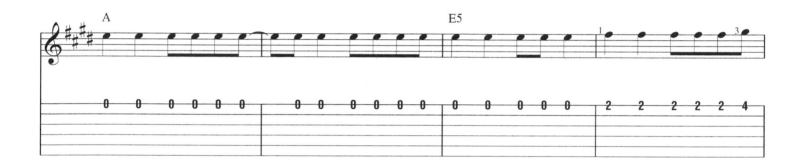
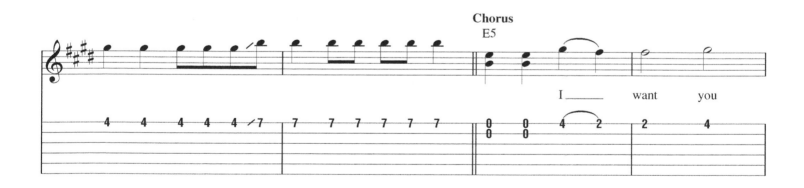

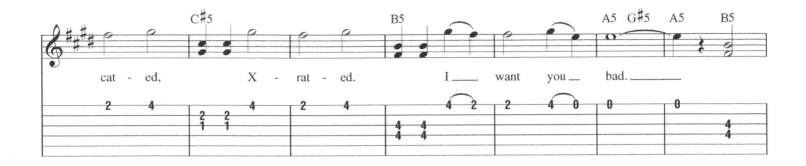

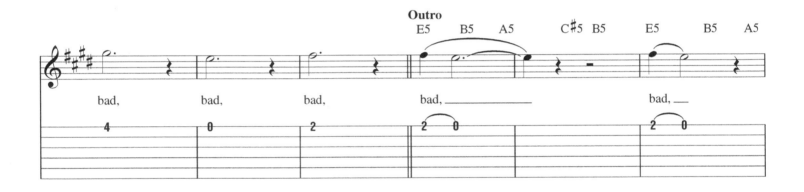

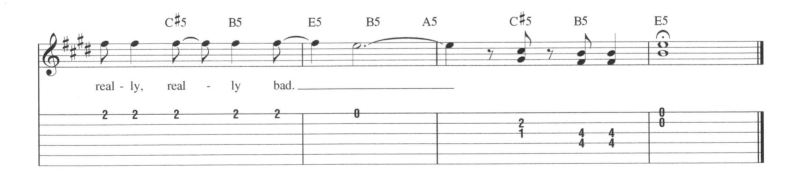

Additional Lyrics

2. If you could only read my mind,
   You would know that I've been waiting so long
   For someone almost just like you,
   But with attitude. I'm waiting, so come on.

Defy You

Words and Music by Dexter Holland

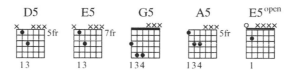

Strum Pattern: 1, 2
Pick Pattern: 2, 4

Intro
Moderately

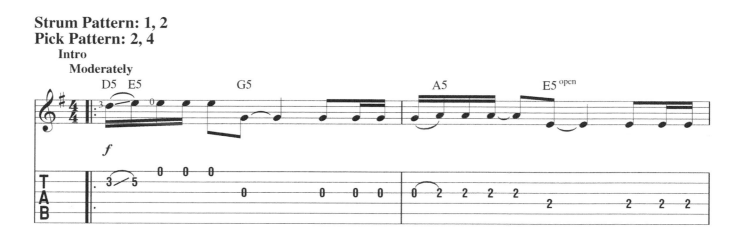

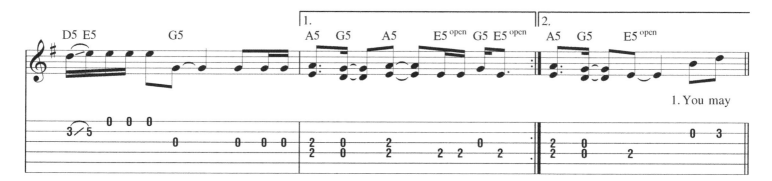

1. You may

Verse

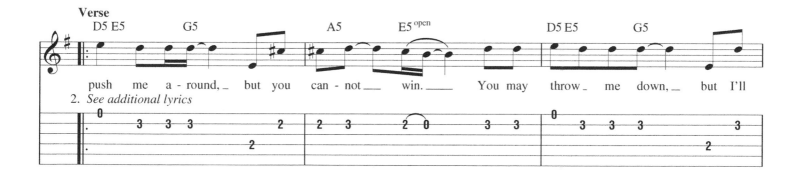

push me a-round, _ but you can-not _ win. _ You may throw _ me down, _ but I'll
2. *See additional lyrics*

rise a - gain. _____ The more _ you say, ___ the more I de-fy you. So get

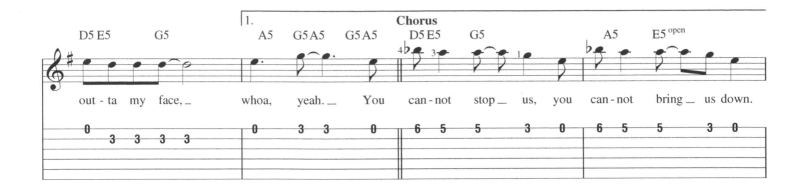

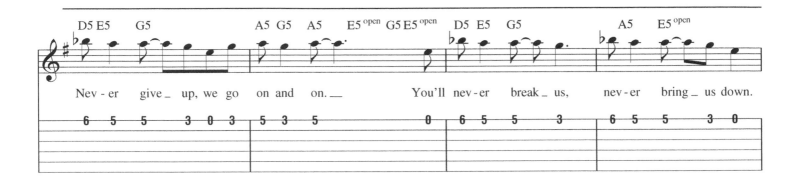

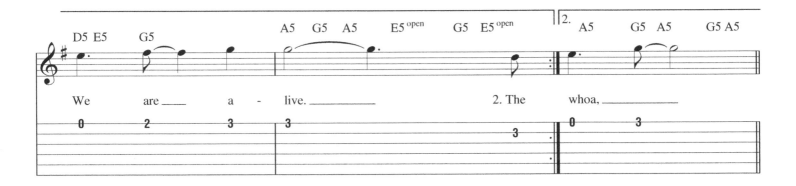

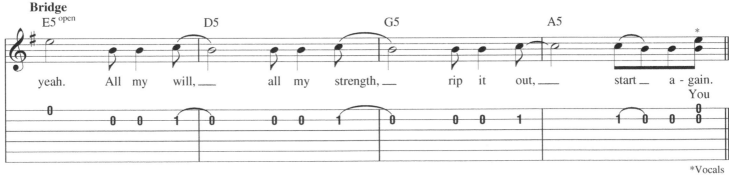

*Vocals
overlap

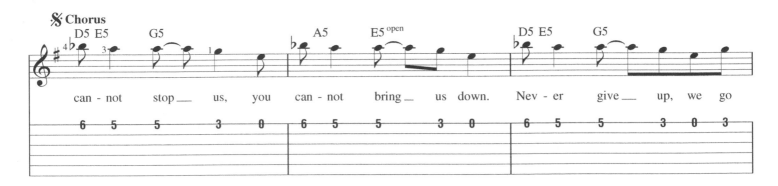

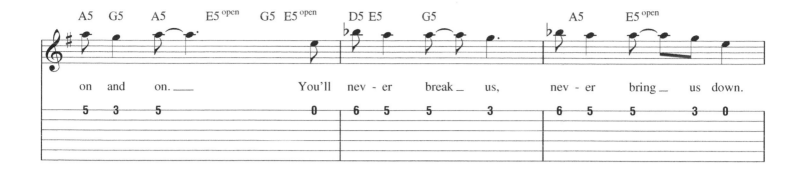

on and on. ___   You'll nev - er break ___ us,   nev - er bring ___ us down.

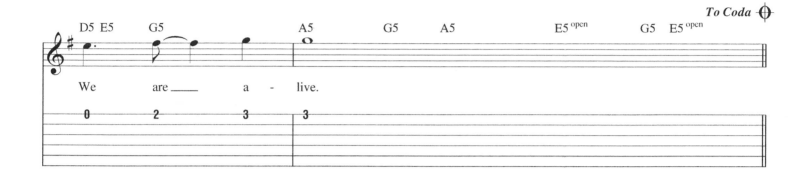

To Coda ⊕

We are ___ a - live.

Guitar Solo

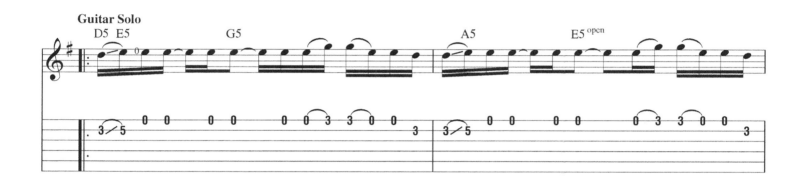

Interlude

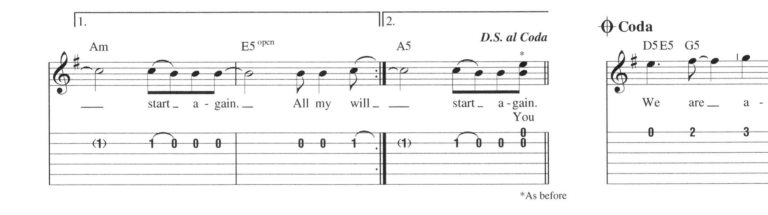

*As before

Additional Lyrics

2. The wind blows, I'll lean into the wind.
   When my anger grows, I'll use it to win.
   The more you say, the more I defy you.
   So get outta my way, whoa, yeah.

Hit That

Words and Music by Dexter Holland

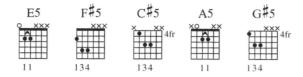

E5 F#5 C#5 A5 G#5

Intro

Moderate Rock

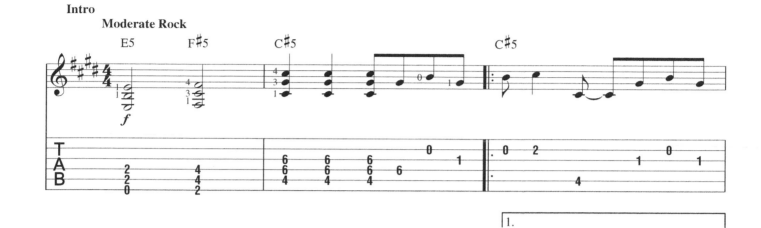

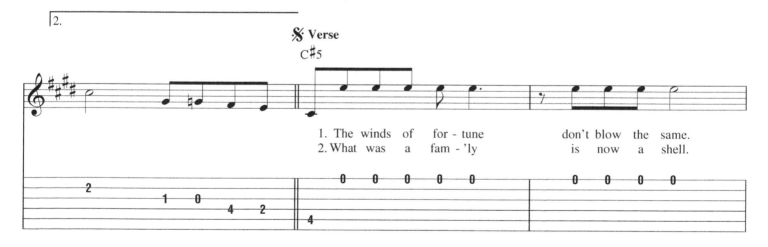

1. The winds of for-tune   don't blow the same.
2. What was a fam-'ly   is now a shell.

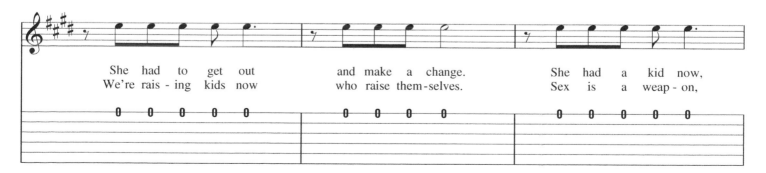

She had to get out   and make a change.   She had a kid now,
We're rais-ing kids now   who raise them-selves.   Sex is a weap-on,

E5   F#5

but much too young.   That ba - by dad-dy's   out hav - ing fun. He's say - ing,
it's like a drug.   It gets him right in - to that grave that he just dug. She's say - ing,

Chorus

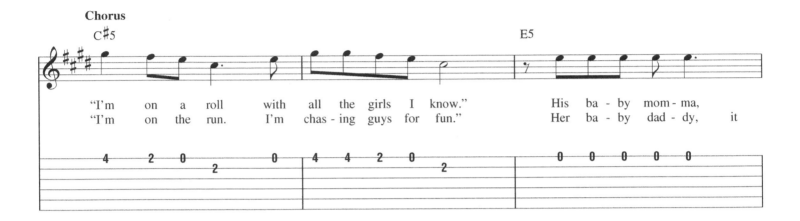

C#5   E5

"I'm on a roll with all the girls I know."   His ba - by mom - ma,
"I'm on the run. I'm chas - ing guys for fun."   Her ba - by dad - dy, it

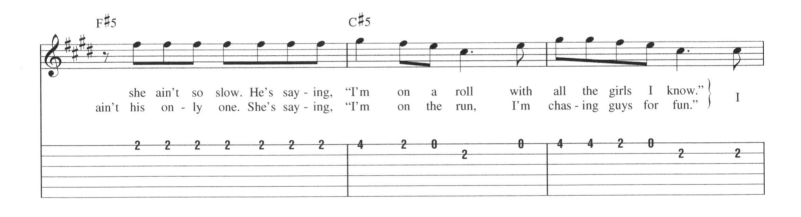

F#5   C#5

she ain't so slow. He's say - ing, "I'm on a roll with all the girls I know."   }   I
ain't his on - ly one. She's say - ing, "I'm on the run, I'm chas - ing guys for fun."   }

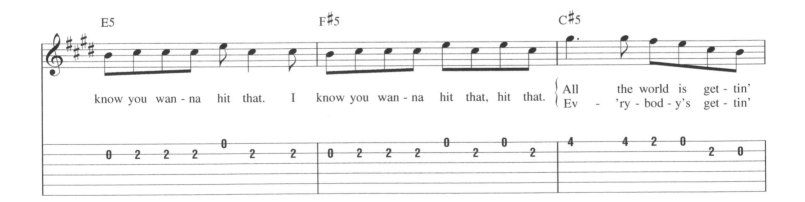

E5   F#5   C#5

know you wan - na hit that. I know you wan - na hit that, hit that.   { All the world is get - tin'
                                                               { Ev - 'ry - bod - y's get - tin'

A5   F#5

with, I say.
with, I say.

Con - se - quenc - es are a lot, but hey.

To Coda

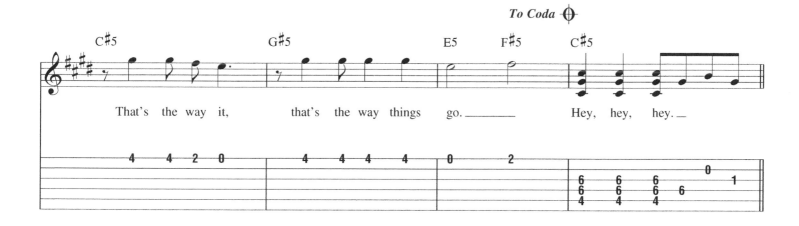

C#5   G#5   E5   F#5   C#5

That's the way it, that's the way things go. _____ Hey, hey, hey. _

Interlude

C#5

D.S. al Coda

C#5

58

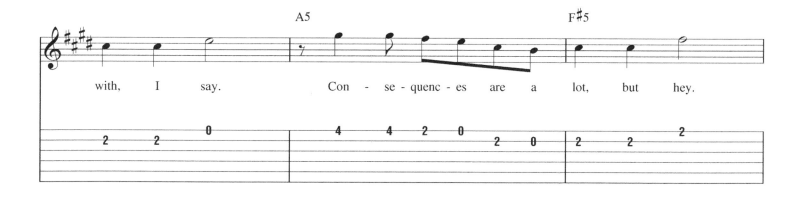

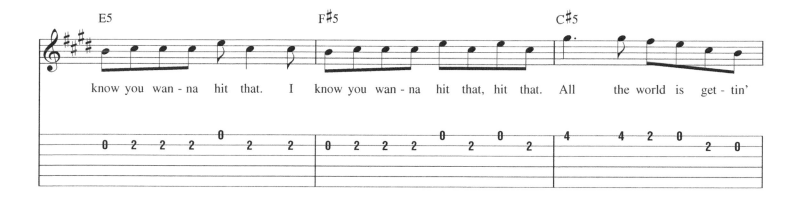

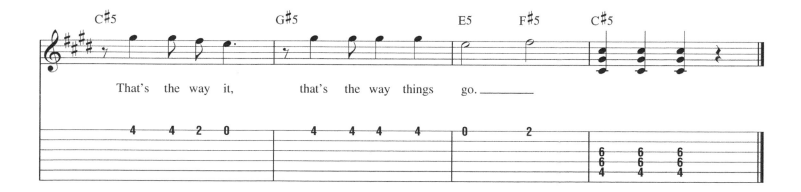

(Can't Get My) Head Around You

Words and Music by Dexter Holland

This series features simplified arrangements with notes, tab, chord charts, and strum and pick patterns.

EASY GUITAR WITH NOTES & TAB

MIXED FOLIOS

00702287	Acoustic	$16.99
00702002	Acoustic Rock Hits for Easy Guitar	$15.99
00702166	All-Time Best Guitar Collection	$19.99
00702232	Best Acoustic Songs for Easy Guitar	$14.99
00119835	Best Children's Songs	$16.99
00702233	Best Hard Rock Songs	$15.99
00703055	The Big Book of Nursery Rhymes & Children's Songs	$16.99
00698978	Big Christmas Collection	$17.99
00702394	Bluegrass Songs for Easy Guitar	$12.99
00289632	Bohemian Rhapsody	$17.99
00703387	Celtic Classics	$14.99
00224808	Chart Hits of 2016-2017	$14.99
00267383	Chart Hits of 2017-2018	$14.99
00334293	Chart Hits of 2019-2020	$16.99
00702149	Children's Christian Songbook	$9.99
00702028	Christmas Classics	$8.99
00101779	Christmas Guitar	$14.99
00702185	Christmas Hits	$10.99
00702141	Classic Rock	$8.95
00159642	Classical Melodies	$12.99
00253933	Disney/Pixar's Coco	$16.99
00702203	CMT's 100 Greatest Country Songs	$29.99
00702283	The Contemporary Christian Collection	$16.99
00196954	Contemporary Disney	$19.99

00702239	Country Classics for Easy Guitar	$22.99
00702257	Easy Acoustic Guitar Songs	$14.99
00702280	Easy Guitar Tab White Pages	$29.99
00702041	Favorite Hymns for Easy Guitar	$10.99
00222701	Folk Pop Songs	$14.99
00126894	Frozen	$14.99
00333922	Frozen 2	$14.99
00702286	Glee	$16.99
00702160	The Great American Country Songbook	$16.99
00267383	Great American Gospel for Guitar	$12.99
00702050	Great Classical Themes for Easy Guitar	$8.99
00702116	Greatest Hymns for Guitar	$10.99
00275088	The Greatest Showman	$17.99
00148030	Halloween Guitar Songs	$14.99
00702273	Irish Songs	$12.99
00192503	Jazz Classics for Easy Guitar	$14.99
00702275	Jazz Favorites for Easy Guitar	$15.99
00702274	Jazz Standards for Easy Guitar	$17.99
00702162	Jumbo Easy Guitar Songbook	$19.99
00232285	La La Land	$16.99
00702258	Legends of Rock	$14.99
00702189	MTV's 100 Greatest Pop Songs	$24.95
00702272	1950s Rock	$15.99
00702271	1960s Rock	$15.99
00702270	1970s Rock	$16.99
00702269	1980s Rock	$15.99

00702268	1990s Rock	$19.99
00109725	Once	$14.99
00702187	Selections from O Brother Where Art Thou?	$19.99
00702178	100 Songs for Kids	$14.99
00702515	Pirates of the Caribbean	$16.99
00702125	Praise and Worship for Guitar	$10.99
00287930	Songs from *A Star Is Born, The Greatest Showman, La La Land,* and More Movie Musicals	$16.99
00702285	Southern Rock Hits	$12.99
00156420	Star Wars Music	$14.99
00121535	30 Easy Celtic Guitar Solos	$15.99
00702156	3-Chord Rock	$12.99
00702220	Today's Country Hits	$12.99
00244654	Top Hits of 2017	$14.99
00283786	Top Hits of 2018	$14.99
00702294	Top Worship Hits	$15.99
00702255	VH1's 100 Greatest Hard Rock Songs	$29.99
00702175	VH1's 100 Greatest Songs of Rock and Roll	$27.99
00702253	Wicked	$12.99

ARTIST COLLECTIONS

00702267	AC/DC for Easy Guitar	$15.99
00702598	Adele for Easy Guitar	$15.99
00156221	Adele – 25	$16.99
00702040	Best of the Allman Brothers	$16.99
00702865	J.S. Bach for Easy Guitar	$14.99
00702169	Best of The Beach Boys	$12.99
00702292	The Beatles — 1	$19.99
00125796	Best of Chuck Berry	$15.99
00702201	The Essential Black Sabbath	$12.95
00702250	blink-182 — Greatest Hits	$16.99
02501615	Zac Brown Band — The Foundation	$19.99
02501621	Zac Brown Band — You Get What You Give	$16.99
00702043	Best of Johnny Cash	$16.99
00702090	Eric Clapton's Best	$12.99
00702086	Eric Clapton — from the Album Unplugged	$15.99
00702202	The Essential Eric Clapton	$15.99
00702053	Best of Patsy Cline	$15.99
00222697	Very Best of Coldplay – 2nd Edition	$14.99
00702229	The Very Best of Creedence Clearwater Revival	$15.99
00702145	Best of Jim Croce	$15.99
00702219	David Crowder*Band Collection	$12.95
00702278	Crosby, Stills & Nash	$12.99
14042809	Bob Dylan	$14.99
00702276	Fleetwood Mac — Easy Guitar Collection	$16.99
00139462	The Very Best of Grateful Dead	$15.99
00702136	Best of Merle Haggard	$14.99
00702227	Jimi Hendrix — Smash Hits	$19.99
00702288	Best of Hillsong United	$12.99
00702236	Best of Antonio Carlos Jobim	$15.99

00702245	Elton John — Greatest Hits 1970–2002	$17.99
00129855	Jack Johnson	$16.99
00702204	Robert Johnson	$12.99
00702234	Selections from Toby Keith — 35 Biggest Hits	$12.95
00702003	Kiss	$16.99
00110578	Best of Kutless	$12.99
00702216	Lynyrd Skynyrd	$16.99
00702182	The Essential Bob Marley	$14.99
00146081	Maroon 5	$14.99
00121925	Bruno Mars – Unorthodox Jukebox	$12.99
00702248	Paul McCartney — All the Best	$14.99
00702129	Songs of Sarah McLachlan	$12.95
00125484	The Best of MercyMe	$12.99
02501316	Metallica — Death Magnetic	$19.99
00702209	Steve Miller Band — Young Hearts (Greatest Hits)	$12.95
00124167	Jason Mraz	$15.99
00702096	Best of Nirvana	$15.99
00702211	The Offspring — Greatest Hits	$12.95
00138026	One Direction	$14.99
00702030	Best of Roy Orbison	$16.99
00702144	Best of Ozzy Osbourne	$14.99
00702279	Tom Petty	$12.99
00102911	Pink Floyd	$16.99
00702139	Elvis Country Favorites	$17.99
00702293	The Very Best of Prince	$16.99
00699415	Best of Queen for Guitar	$15.99
00109279	Best of R.E.M.	$14.99
00702208	Red Hot Chili Peppers — Greatest Hits	$16.99
00198960	The Rolling Stones	$16.99
00174793	The Very Best of Santana	$14.99
00702196	Best of Bob Seger	$15.99

00146046	Ed Sheeran	$17.99
00702252	Frank Sinatra — Nothing But the Best	$17.99
00702010	Best of Rod Stewart	$16.99
00702049	Best of George Strait	$14.99
00702259	Taylor Swift for Easy Guitar	$15.99
00254499	Taylor Swift – Easy Guitar Anthology	$19.99
00702260	Taylor Swift — Fearless	$14.99
00139727	Taylor Swift — 1989	$17.99
00115960	Taylor Swift — Red	$16.99
00253667	Taylor Swift — Reputation	$17.99
00702290	Taylor Swift — Speak Now	$16.99
00702223	Chris Tomlin—Arriving	$16.99
00232849	Chris Tomlin Collection – 2nd Edition	$12.95
00702226	Chris Tomlin — See the Morning	$12.95
00148643	Train	$14.99
00702427	U2 — 18 Singles	$16.99
00702108	Best of Stevie Ray Vaughan	$16.99
00279005	The Who	$14.99
00702123	Best of Hank Williams	$15.99
00194548	Best of John Williams	$14.99
00702111	Stevie Wonder — Guitar Collection	$9.95
00702228	Neil Young — Greatest Hits	$15.99
00119133	Neil Young — Harvest	$14.99

Prices, contents and availability subject to change without notice.

Visit Hal Leonard online at **halleonard.com**